Forever Faithful

Aunt Elaine & Uncle Oscar,
Thank you for helping
shape me into the person
that I am today.
I appreciate you for help
raising me as a young
child. "Never let fear
over power your dreams"
Love, Michelle Rose Welch
XOXOXO

Forever Faithful

Michelle Rose Welch

ISBN: Hardcover   978-1-4363-6211-5
               Softcover   978-1-4363-6210-8

This book was printed in the United States of America.

To order additional copies of this book, contact:
Xlibris Corporation
1-888-795-4274
www.Xlibris.com
Orders@Xlibris.com
50700

Table Of Contents

Dedications

This book is dedicated to my most treasured people. I can't possibly name them all one by one, But I can share a few.

First, I would like to say "Thank you and I love you" to my supportive husband. He has inspired me tremendously throughout our entire marriage. If it weren't for my husband, I would never have had the courage to publish this book. He helped me focus on my dreams, near and far. He had faith in me, when I had no faith in myself.

Secondly, I'd like to say "I love you" to my mother. She always told me that I could do anything if I put my mind to it. She inspired me growing up, As she was always a strong, independent woman. She taught me to be myself and not be afraid of what others might think. She is my hero and my dear friend.

Thirdly, I'd like to say "Thank you for being you" to my Aunt Cheryl. She has always been there for me when I needed a friendly ear to listen. She has inspired me in so many ways, Mostly spiritually. She has always lifted my spirits and my heart when I was feeling down. Even when she had breast cancer, she was so refreshing to be around. No matter how bad off she was, She would never dwell on the negatives.

Last, but not least, I'd like to thank my daughter. She has inspired me more than she'll ever know. Just one look into her blue eyes, And I just melt away like butter. She is the most exquisite, little girl I have ever seen. I'm so proud to be the mother of such a wonderful, and darling baby girl.

So many others have played an inspiring role in my life. Some people were not good people, but they inspired me to let my feelings out on paper. Others have simply been very helpful to me while I was learning how to jot my feelings down. For those people, good and bad, I'm very gracious for the experiences that were given to me.

Foreword

Writing is a form of art. You can release your inner feelings out on paper. Poetry can get you through a lot of hard times in your life. Anyone can be a writer, But many people don't realize their own talents. Sometimes we don't understand the poetry that we read. Each of us interpret things differently, Since each of us see things differently. Writers are people who express themselves as best they can. Don't be afraid to express yourself and be yourself. Trust in your heart, And you shall not fail.

FOREVER FAITHFUL BLISS

For those who love many things in life.

"Forever faithful"

Splashing around in my own pool of doubt
I wondered how I could live with you
Then, I wondered how I could live without
I was merely so blind to this whole love thing at first
After that one special kiss
I needed more
As if I was dying of thirst
You were like a thief in the night
Stealing my innocent heart away
I was so scared
I didn't know how to act
Or what to say
I had been pondering over a broken heart for years
I wanted to let some sunshine in
Instead of more tears
I have found that the love bug spreads new life
That is why now I have gotten over my fears
And I have become your forever faithful wife

"As love grows"

How gracious I feel to be with you
Look how our love got more confident
Everyone can see how it grew
Our love is like a vine that keeps growing taller
We kept up our faith when we were much smaller
We are kindred hearts combined as one
Our life isn't always candy apples and fun
We have to work as a team to keep our lives up beat
I'll massage your back
And You can rub my feet
Together we can make this all work out
Let's erase any bad thoughts or doubts
I want to still be with you as my hair turns gray
I will devote my whole life to you
We will be together until our dying day
I'll never forget our first shy kiss
My heart gave a sigh of pure loves bliss
When we argue, We need to remember certain things
We took our vows, And exchanged gold rings
I wish for everyone to feel this elation
We need to pass along the love bug
Then the world can have the most fulfilling celebration

"Noble Man"

Noble is the man in the mask
He fights with pride and integrity
He will never turn down a job or task
He doesn't mind a little sweat above his brow
He always finishes his work and does his chores before eating chow
The woman he loves is very impatient
But she's beautiful and when she sees him
She's filled with such heartfelt elation
She misses her man who fights for what's right
She is extremely lonely and emotional at night
He writes to her everyday
She writes back with so much to say
They converse back and fourth through their letters
She pours out her fragile heart
She then asks
Will you be home by May?
What a blessing that would be
To have her Noble man she loves back home for her to again see

"Two People In Love"

I didn't want to come out of my comfort zone
I had always got by so well on my own
How could I resist his handsome face
It wasn't long before I invited him over to my place
His smile just lit up the whole room
Now I knew my heart was doomed
I was in for a royal treat
He looked at me, and I was swept right off of my feet
I fell so far, Super fast
It wasn't long after meeting that he asked
The big question that is
I said yes, And we went from there
We have been told, We are the most heavenly pair
The two of us created another being
In our eyes, It is only love that we are seeing

We may argue every now and then
But, We are more happy now, than way back when
Our lives have changed so very much
I wouldn't trade a single minute or even a touch
The three of us are content as can be
Just watch from a distance and you shall see
Family is extremely important to us
You need people in your lives that you can really trust
It all starts with two people in love

Believe in the freedom

Cradle my head for support
I need you to keep me well
My knees are skinned and sore
I will polish my nails when I get bored
I forgive those who frown down upon my face
I will weep due to ill words that people say
Maybe I can make them nice one day
I just need to meditate and pray
Bundle my cold arms up next to yours
Look into my gleaming eyes
Catch me now before my tears start to pour
Don't be scared of what you don't understand
Be brave and take a strong hold of my fragile hand
I will lead you to the place where your heart can be free
Sit right down and stare directly at me
Brush my hair with a tender stroke of your hand
We can kneel in the soft, warm sand
Take a deep breath and count to three
The breeze carries you away
Right to where your heart needs to be

"Engage my heart"

Body and soul
I feel the tenderness on my skin
He loves me I know
My feelings and hopes I want to show
I need this man in my life
I want him to make me his forever faithful wife
I will wait a lifetime
If that is how long I have to wait
He is my inspiration
My love, my fate
I can't live without this man of mine
He makes me feel wonderful
I need him until the end of time
He makes me feel special and cared for
He will soon open a new door
The door is our future
I hold him dear to my heart
No one now can tear our love apart
We are a team
We will soon be one
He is my sky, moon and sun
He is my partner in everything we do
Hey baby, I love you!!!

"Our own way"

Ecstatic I was to see him again
My heart was the first thing he had to win
I know loving him can't be wrong or be a sin
We are one in our hearts and one within
Our love grows stronger every waking moment
We have proclaimed ourselves in front of God
There are no secrets or stories untold
We believe in trust in our house hold
We speak our minds and speak our hearts
We won't go down without a fight
We try to keep focused
We don't want to lose our destination
We don't want to ever lose sight
Burning, my skin feels lying next to him
My excitement takes me on a new high
Thrilled my senses become when he touches my arm
I get chills and let out a quiet sigh
He simply nudges my hand and I become paralyzed
Our eyes slow dance in their own little way
We don't even talk
Our eyes know what to say
We have our own language
We could be silent all day
In our hearts we know what is going on
We are giddy and humming our own song
Others may laugh and think we are wrong
We plan for eternity and life together
Forever our love shall be
Parting, we will never see
On our cloud of a fluffy heart
Just try to pull or tug
You won't be able to tear us apart

"The woman"
"The angel"

Sing with the angels
Adore the woman
Fly under my wings
Dream about the woman
Shower me with gold
Dance with the angels
Taste the clouds
Ever so fluffy
Furious roses
Drooling over the grass
Meet with the angels
Seek the woman
Travel with the angels
Sights you may see
Pick the tulips
Don't you speak
Open your eyes

Fly so very high
Play with the angels
Caress the woman
Soft as cotton
Mild and meek
Whisper to the angels
Quiet voices
Romance the woman
Lay down upon a cloud
Make love to the woman

"I do"

Return my call before it turns dark
If it's not too late, We can meet at the park
The moon I hear will be dull tonight
I like it better when it is shiny and bright
Let's hold hands while we walk in silence
I want to walk for miles and miles
When we finally stop to talk
There are several things I need to say to you
My heart pumps and beats and it wants to say "I do"
I get shaky and tremble with every touch
You mean the world to me
You just don't know how very much
I can't live without you near
I'm so glad you decided to meet me here
We belong in the same boat together
Let's sail away and be one forever

"Chloe"

Little angel
Blow your bubbles
Skin like velvet
Eyes blue like the sky
Disposition is sweet like pie
Sassy smile
Beautiful face
No one could ever take her place
She's my number one
We will always play and have so much fun
Rosy cheeks
Soft and sweet
Love so pure
If you're ever sad or blue
She will be your cure
Shiny like a bright gem
Precious as a doll
Smart like her parents
She's really got it all

I love my angel baby, Chloe Alexis

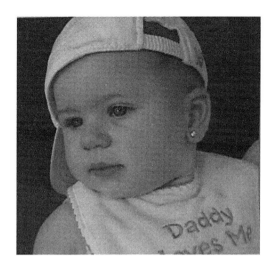

"Angel Blue Eyes"

Her piercing blue eyes
They gaze into mine
She's a little princess in training
Her heart is pure and divine
She has wings and one day she will fly
High above the birds and clouds
Way on up into the sky
Her cheeks are rosy and kind of chubby
She's my protective cherub
My special doll baby
My best little friend
She's my heart until the very end
I love her oh so much
I cherish her soft skin
She is velvety to the touch
Tender smooth kisses
She lands them upon my cheek

We play games
One of them is hide and go seek
I plan to take good care of her
At least until she is all grown
At that point I will let her go out on her own
I will trust she learned all that I had known
I will give her space to make up her own mind
She is so brilliant
She is my angel baby who is one of a kind

"My little girl"

Strong chocolate breath laughs in my face
She's so precious
No one could take her place
She's rambunctious and curious
She never meets a stranger
She is sometimes overly friendly
She is too young to know of the danger
Her scent is baby powder and lavender lotion
She smells so nice
I wouldn't trade her for all the pearls in the ocean
My baby girl and cute little friend
I will give her my love until the very end
She is sacred and beloved to me
She pulls her daddy's glasses off his head
She laughs loudly
Poor daddy
He can't see

It's surely funny to watch them play
I would love it to forever stay this way
But I know one day she'll be all grown
My heart will start to unravel
I'll need to stitch it back
I will keep it sewn
As it starts to come undone again
I'll have to think back to the way things had always been
Her soft blonde hair
I start to twirl
No matter what
She'll always be my little girl

"The Screaming Beauty"

She screams so loud
My heart wants to give out
I pray for her to go to sleep
She gets even louder, As I take a peak
Sometimes she makes it rough for me to stay sane
If I don't get any sleep, I'll be on La La lane
I keep telling myself she's only a baby
We'll get through this awkward stage
I have to stay confident and have courage
I know John and I will do great
I hope she only takes on our good traits
Right now she is very strong willed
With laughter and smiles, My heart is filled
I cherish those special glances that she gives me
They are the most brilliant, Anyone can see

She glows even when she is throwing a fit
Even still, When I put her in the corner to sit
John and I will work our magic to make her understand
She is a child, We are her parents
We most definitely have the upper hand
Love, we for sure will pass it down
For now, I need to pick her up off of the ground
She is pitching herself another royal fit
We love her no matter what
That's all we know to do, That's it

"Baby Steps"

Speak my beautiful name
Does it sound at all the same?
Is this just a silly, unspoken game?
I want to be yours
Try to set your soul free
Be who you want to be
Take another step towards me
I want to be your destination
Come a little closer and you'll see
One baby step at a time
Ring my bells
I will hear them chime
We could run away with the circus
We could drive a school bus
Whatever we do, I want to do it with you
Are you a man who is for real?
If you are, Show me how you feel
If you feel blue, You don't need to whine
I will take your sorrow away, Then you'll be fine
Speak those words that you could never define
How sweet you are
You finally gave me a real sign
Now I truly know
You had always been mine

BROKEN
HEART
ROWE

For anyone who has ever had a broken heart.

"Why so hard"?

Why is everything so hard to do?
Why do things in life make me so blue?
I just want to be recognized for what I have done
All of my strength seems to be gone
I struggle with my pride every day
I have said all of the things I needed to say
My heart seems to be leaping through steamy fire
I sink into the black hole that I do not desire
I scribble my notes on my left hand
I try and find a quiet place to land
My tears well up in my sad green eyes
No one feels my pain or hears my cries
I used to smile all day long
Now I catch myself singing depressing songs
Why did they not believe my words?
They might as well come at me with stabbing swords
I said my prayers and I said my part
Now I will just have faith with all of my heart

"Lies"

Don't tell me anymore of your lies
You are such a good salesman
I bet you could sell a bag full of flies
You have cheated my heart one too many times
I can see you even trying to sell lemons for limes
You don't make any sense at all
You're a vicious person, think back and try to recall
The things you have done
I'm out the door, I'm really gone
You don't deserve me or my love
I will take it all back, I will fly away like a dove
I trusted you and your bogus story
Oh, now you want to leave
What is the real hurry?
Did I catch you in some covered up schemes?
Go ahead and run
As you whisk away, I will unravel you at the seams
They say, The truth shall set you free
I'm glad I was honest
Because now I can see, You weren't meant for me

"Heartbreak"

My angry heart thumps so loud
Beats so strong
I've been done so wrong
I will cry once more
Will no one hear me?
My heart aches and is sore
My emotions weaken day by day
I feel I have no more to say
A roller coaster would be more fun
I lay on my back to see the sun
I struggle to smirk or smile
To be so pale is not my style
I have been stricken from my own life or mind
I feel I'm being left far behind
White is beautiful and so is black
All I want is my own life back
My heart is beating louder than before
Soon if I'm not careful
I'll be knockin on heavens door
My heart can only take so much pain
I want to live long enough to see one more rain

"Get Away"

Smug as a thief
Before he hit her
She had such beautiful teeth
Her smile had faded away
She was scared of him each and every day
He would brag to friends about being so bad
Telling people he was the best thing that she ever had
Things started to turn sour
Day by day and hour by grueling hour
She was being eaten up by fear
He would hit her
Smack her around
Then call her baby and dear
What could she do?
Just run for her precious life?
She endured so much heartache, pain and strife
One day she will get away
Until then, she will meditate and pray
She will soon be free
No longer will she be captive and blinded
She will be willing and able to again see

"Not gonna settle"

Why did they lie?
Why do I cry?
Why does this whole thing cut me down to size?
How do I get back up after falling down?
No one will lend me a friendly hand.
How did my heart get so wrenched?
I've been discarded like garbage.
Can they not see my pain?
I guess I have to make a ruckus or raise some cain.
I want my life back in order.
I just want to be myself again and be somewhat sane.
I've lost my inner fight.
I have let certain things out of my sight.
Should I settle for this?
Who knows? I just might.
I can't take much more of this scrambling in my head.
I feel like I'm frying bacon and eggs.
My tears want to pour.
I'm getting close to where I can't take much more.
They have stripped me down to my bare soul.
I have fallen into the devil's hole.
I know I need to be strong.
I know I need to fight for what is right.
I know I shouldn't take this too light.
I need to step up once again.
Telling the truth is not a sin.
I will proceed with my eyes wide open.
I shouldn't just be hoping.
I need to realize this is for real.
The truth shall prevail and I will be set free.
I will score the all time ultimate deal.

"Abuse"

Abuse
That's what I've seen
That's what I've felt
That's what I've heard
It was hard to adjust to it all
After a while, it became second nature
I saw it
I felt it
I heard it
The pain was unreal
The sight was cruel
The feeling was nauseating
The words so disturbing and crushing to my heart
Mental anguish was harder to deal with than physical pain
Sometimes I felt like a rag doll that was all used up
Every now and then, I feel that pain
I get flashbacks of the sight of anger
The feelings of rage
The harsh words of hate
I will never get over my sorrow
I will have to move on and look forward to tomorrow

"Run"

Help her
Help her run
Help her run away
Help her run away from him
He beats her
She weeps on her knees
He tore her insides right out of her
He left her begging for mercy
Please, God
Show her some mercy
No one deserves this kind of abuse
She has always helped others
She needs to find her strength within
Pull deep from your very soul
God will show you mercy
Follow the path he has chosen for you
Your soul is beautiful and you are too

"Family against one"

Does he want to die?
Why does he not care if we cry?
Does he not understand our pain and why?
Our hearts are hurting with each beat
We just want him to stand on his own two feet
He abuses his body with drugs and alcohol
He gets angry when we try to help
He yells at us and makes us feel so small
Why doesn't he know how to stop?
We intervene at times and it ends up being a big flop
He storms out of the room with anger in mind
He doesn't realize that good family is hard to find
We care and that is why we try so hard
We beg him to stay away from the bars
One day he might hurt another being
His eyes get blurred and double vision is what he is seeing
I beg and plea for him not to leave
The door slams and he is gone in the night
I want to help him, I don't want to fight
I have done all that I could to see him get well
Will he ever be better?
Only his lifestyle change and time can tell

"The wife"

I fight the tears
I struggle with my pride
I keep things hidden
I just seem to flow with the tide
My heart is high upon a shelf
I feel like I'm not quite my old self
I want to cry
But I feel that I'll seem too weak
My blood rises up to the sky
My illusions chase me like a butterfly
My veins pound through my thin, silky skin
My hair continues to fall out
But I can never give in
I need to let my feelings out
Instead I stand in the corner and just pout
I used to love my happy go lucky life
Now I'm feeling down
I feel I have failed at being a good wife
Can I ever get my charm back in me
Maybe one day I can explain
And maybe one day my heart will be set free

"Child Abuse"

Lost little girl trying to find her way
Thinking of how to act every single day
She will be smacked really hard across the face
Quiet she remains most of her days
Writing gets her through so many things
Her mother and father abuse her body and mind
She is the best little girl, She is one of a kind
She smiles with bruises upon her cheek
She is so brave and yet so mild and meek
She must clean all of the floors on her knees
God, Look after this angel child please
Her heart is so heavy and yet she is so light
She sees past all the negativity, She is so bright
Her arms are folded tightly across her chest
She wants to be saved from this time of test
This poor girl needs a bed to lay in and rest
Her parents push her to be the maid around the home
They sit on there butts and slouch on there thrones
Her teacher notices her new bruises today
Will she cover up for her parents again?
What might she say?
She will tell the truth finally this time
They will go to jail for doing such a hideous crime
Justice shall prevail in this young girls life
She will no longer struggle to survive

"Tunnel Vision"

Scared again
Wishing on that glowing star
Holding back thoughts
I can't seem to go very far
My emotions running away from me
Leaping away from what I don't want to see
Grinding my teeth late at night
I just want to live
I don't like to fight
I can be happy
But only in dreams
Nothing in reality is really what it seems
I gaze into the tunnel of truth
I see myself
But not in my youth
My windows are shattered
My heart is on fire
And my mind is all scattered

ODYSSEY
OF
ORIGINALITY

For the many eccentric ideas that have formed in my head.

"Pink"

Sunset dreams, filled by moonlit screams
Nothing at all, Is what it seems
Being plain me, Is the way I like to be
Pink flowers dancing in the sun
They are beautiful all day
Playing and having such fun
Chasing fireflies into the sky
The angels seem to glide right by
Tossing and turning all night long
Somehow feeling worthless, and lonely
Have I done everything all wrong?
Make me smile once again
I want to be free of all hate and any sin
Let me dive into the light, I will then see
Having my senses return, Then I see the new sight.

"Bamboo of fear"

Bamboo is hard to walk through
Fire surrounds us
The smoke makes it hard to breathe
It's so quiet
The wind stopped
There is no movement
No sound
Whisper in my ear
Shall you spread the silent words
Feel the curse all around us
Face our fears
Scary voices are all I hear
Tie your shoes
Run as fast as you can
Make some noise now
I need to feel alive
I've been close to death for a long time
We begin to shout out for help
Bamboo is starting to crumble
See the sadness of their whelps
Will my cries be heard?
To many captives
This may seem absurd
They don't understand my life
They haven't tasted my tears
All I know
I want my soul back
I want to finally face my inner fears

"Mannerisms"

Twirling my hair around my index finger
Tapping my feet on the cold tile floor
Bobbing my right leg up and down
Grinding my teeth from side to side
Scratching my nose out of control
Smacking my gum obnoxiously loud
Pampering a young child's ego
Writing with a pen that is leaking
Talking too softly for anyone to hear me
Wearing my pajamas all day long
Taking pictures of the silliest stuff in sight
Laughing at the most non funny jokes
Having pain throughout my whole body
Spasms that last for hours on end
Having gas from eating something greasy
Clapping about something I saw on television
Chasing two dogs around the house
Snoring at night with my mouth wide open
Kissing my husband with drool coming down
Snorting at a joke that was really funny
Crying at a lifetime movie that was sad
These are my mannerisms
Some are good and some are bad
Some are just things I can't help
I wouldn't trade a single thing
With each day, I'm proud to be me and I'm so glad

"Wow"

The high fence is blocking my view
I'm trying to check out my neighbor
I want to welcome him, because he's new
I'll go to his door and shake his hand
I have to be perky, I don't want to seem bland
Gorgeous he looks from far away
Nice view, It will be great to see this every day
Handsome, strong legs he has from this spot
I will give him the cookies that I just got
Maybe he will be tender and sweet
I want a man to knock me off my feet
I love guys that can tell a joke
I don't want a guy who likes to smoke
I need to just go over and meet him
I'll go grab the cookie tin
On my way, I will head there now
Uh oh, I see a woman and wow!!!!
She is walking up to him and kissing his lips
She even knows how to shake her hips
I better turn around and head back home
I feel silly now, Like a funny looking gnome
The alarm clock goes off, And now I'm awake
Oh my, That was just a dream
That would have been awful, For heavens sake
I look out my window and that man is for real
He is moving in to the house next to Mrs. Teal
I see no woman in sight, Should I go over?
You never know, I just might

"To be young again"

I chuckled about a funny joke last night
It seemed to make me laugh like I was out of my mind
I haven't smiled like that since I was a young child
My heart did a horse like giddy up
Now my life is more grown up and rough
Cheerful, I would love to be again
The last time I was, I think I was ten
Sugar cookies and apple dumplings
The silly songs we used to sing
I miss the good ole' days of playing outside
My friends and I would run and hide
Yummy, My momma's food tasted every night
Her freshly cooked green beans were out of sight
I enjoyed walking home from school
I would be sweaty and then I jumped right in the pool
I was so hyper and full of life
Now I'm a stressed out mother and wife
I would never change my life as it is today
I wouldn't trade my memories no matter what I say
Good or bad, I love them all
I do however miss playing kick ball
But what I miss most, is being young and small

"Some People"

Frenzied and out of control
Clever and yet has no soul
High but feeling so low
Tough and yet feels so soft
Housed but sleeps only in a loft
Sweet but acts so mean
Trashy but really is super clean
Heavy but used to be light
Too big and yet feels so tight
Grounded but seems so morose
So distant and yet so very close
Hectic but at the same time so calm
Lipstick lover but wears lip balm
Sugary and yet so sour
Loves clocks but doesn't know the hour
Troubled but so very stable
Sits at a lounge bar instead of a table
Reads but doesn't like to look at a book
Food sassy but won't even cook
What a tragic blow
Does this seem like anyone you know?
Some people don't make any sense
They may say or do one thing and really mean another
That is how the world will be always and forever

"Swept Away"

Mystical waves crash in my mind
I stand alone, I reach for you
But I'm too far behind
I will sit in silence
I will enjoy the rain, It pours down
As I run from going insane
You once held me up to the sky
I bowed down, And you started to cry
I was locked up tight in a cage
I didn't see any black
I only saw myself in a shade of sage
Sand starts to hit me hard in the face
As the wind kicks up, I start to run
But only in place, I don't seem to move
I just stay there, In my dreams
My life seems not at all fair
Taste the drops coming from above
All I ever desired was beautiful, unconditional love
The clouds begin to race forward
They are going so quick, They need to slow down
I'm becoming dizzy, And feeling sick
Come to me in my dreams
I will make you laugh so hard
You will burst your pants at the seams
Trust me on this lovely ocean
You will soon see
I will be out of my cage and with you
Forever happy again and free

"Goodbye Work"
"Hello World"

I'm so happy
Yet I'm so sad
Missing things I used to have
I miss my work
I miss the uniforms I had
My life has changed
But that's not all so bad
I'm now a little girls Grandad
I need to stay strong
I want to be with my family where I belong
My work was so great
But now I have moved on to my next fate
I will miss all of the good times
As well as the trying times too
I'm proud of all the wonderful people I once knew
We were a family

We were a team
I will have to strum up a new scheme
My life won't be dull or boring
I will keep busy as a bee
I will take care of my family, you'll see
They make me so complete
My memories and friends
I will always keep in my heart with me
So, I won't cry or be upset
I will cherish the special people
Those special ones
I never will forget

* Written for my father in-law, Clinton Welch*

"Will I be great?"

Dizziness and clouds
Fog up my mind
Will I be great?
Or, will I fall behind?
Skies seem bleak
My sanity and happiness I seek
Tired and hungry for new life
Will I be sluggish?
Or, will I be a great wife?
Babies will cry
Will I get angry?
Or, will I hold my hands up and sigh
My head is full of doubt
Will I be strong?
Or, will my heart plum give out?
Honesty and trust
Will I believe?
Oh yes, I must

"My pictures"
"My memories"

My pictures are scattering in the wind
Run, Catch as many as you can
Those are my memories flying away
My heart will be broken if they parish
The window was left ajar
My pictures were on the shelf near by
No, I can't have this happen to me
I run faster, I jump in the air
I'm chasing my memories in circles
I see one of John when he was five
Now I see one of me when I was twenty
The happiness these pictures bring me
I caught a few just now
I think a couple of them got swept far away
I cherish my special memories
Without these pictures, I will not die
I can survive the pain of losing them
All of my memories are in my mind
I have captured those pictures in a still frame in my head
They shall never leave me
My brain has captured many memories to hold
Just because we lose something dear to us
We always have it with us in our hearts and minds
It may be a tragedy at the time to lose it
But, We are blessed in so many ways
We were able to once enjoy those special memories
We can enjoy those memories all over, when we remember
Always remember

"Our Eyes"

Miserable the man appears to be
Perhaps I will cheer him up
I will crack a joke to make him smile
Sir, Why do you frown and look so blue?
He never replies to me
Can't he hear me, Or even see?
I have come to realize he is deaf and blind
I knew he didn't look very happy
But, Who should I be to judge his feelings?
He could be the happiest man alive
You never really know how someone feels
He may not have been able to communicate with me
But, I'm sure someone knows how to get his attention
Here comes a nice looking lady
She sits down beside this man on the park bench
They begin to hold hands
I guess they know each other
She signs in his hand, He seems to understand
He signs back in her hand
I have seen a miracle in the making
How wonderful for this miserable looking man
He actually seems to be smiling now
I think that is so great
The lady is so patient
I know now, Things aren't always what they seem
They begin to kiss
The lady says that she's in love with him
I'm glad that he could find love without seeing
We take our eyes for granted
We really should not go by appearances anyway
She has a heart of gold
And he is the buried treasure that she has been looking for
She sees the real him and takes the time to care
Two hearts were connected with only hands and lips

"Speed Demons"

Speed demon drives way too fast
Frenzied over things from the past
Sliver and slide
Cut your life short if you don't abide
Scary at times in the drivers seat
Hold onto your britches
Put the peddle to your feet
The angels say "Slow Down"
They don't want to see your body lying cold on the ground
Sad, everyone will be
If they have to go to your funeral and loudly grieve
Lots of people die each year
We need more safety
Definintly, not more fear
Listen to your angel that speaks softly to you
Then you will know exactly what you should not do

"Me"

For who am I?
My eyes glance up
Then I'm touching the sky
I'm so high off the ground
The air is thick
I can't even hear a sound
My heart beats faster by the minute
For who am I?
For what is my life without you in it?
I would be nothing once more
For who am I?
I will not open an old scolded door
The sky is my limit
I shall come back down

The air is some thinner
I can start to hear some sound
My high is almost over
My cloud less fun
For who am I?
What have I done?
I have chosen to be me
And this is who I have come to be
For who am I?
Just me

"Wild girls"

In my neighborhood, I use to see rainbow swirls
Now I see my neighbor and her mischievous little girls
They have crazy long eyelashes
They bat them at the guys next door
Pretty curls dangle down their cheek
Most girls are mild and meek
These girls are not like others
They don't have a father
He left one day without a note
He packed a suitcase and grabbed his coat
All they know is how to flirt with danger
Unfortunately they don't know any better
Their mother drinks all day long
She's so messed up all the time
She doesn't realize what her girls are doing wrong
Until their mother finds some help
They are doomed by this life in which they were dealt
I pray for this family to find hope and peace
Help them God, please

"Be"

I joke, I laugh
I smile, I smirk
I wink, I blink
I have fun, I mope around at home
I dance, I prance
I pony up to the bar
I tease, I taunt
I glow, I flaunt
I eat, I sleep
I tend to pick at my feet
I'm just me
That is all I came here to be

"Yourself"

Bonk on the head
Don't drop til your dead
Sing a song, like your momma said
Put together the words that haven't yet been read
Chime the clock just one more time
Think hard before you commit a crime
Turn the pages to your lifeless book
Stay at the bed and breakfast
Sit at the private nook
I won't let you get away
I won't let you off the hook
The pink car pulls up to the driveway
I wonder what it has to say
Talk is cheap
Your words seem deep
My heart will soon ache and weep
Dance with the wave
So many lives we cannot save
Blindfold me and tie me to a chair
Please leave me dressed
Not left just in my underwear
Push yourself to the limit
Don't you wait for even one more minute
Tell your secret out loud
Don't hide behind a mask or shroud
Be yourself
And always be proud

INSPIRATIONAL HIGHWAY

To be inspired, Or just to feel refreshed.

"Brave Within"

Toss the coin into the fountain
You can sit and watch your life go by
Or you can get up and climb a tall mountain
Be brave and believe in yourself
Don't ever be embarrassed or ashamed to ask for help
The birds fly high up in the sky
Keep your composure and don't start to cry
Be strong when things get tough
Life isn't easy, in fact it's quite rough
Find your strength from deep within
Be you and nobody else
That is definintly not a sin

"Serenity"

Don't take your life for granted
Let people help navigate you
Go on a harvesting journey
Seek many new ideas
Catch a falling star
Make the effort to inspire others
Travel across the high seas
Chase the grey shadows that haunt you
Wave towards the lighthouse
God will lead you to the ship of desire
The sun shall revolve around your perky cheeks
No need to quiver or tremble with fear
Follow me, We will arrive soon
When we dream, We can be anywhere we want
If you become frail, I will carry you
There is the sunny valley straight ahead
We can rest before it storms
The seagulls are flying over our heads
Serene, And content you should feel
I wish for you to be just as windswept as myself
Don't hide under a rock
Transform your faith into mighty powers

"Our King"

The cross stands alone
We kiss his feet after washing them
Beautiful roses drape down the side of his robe
He belongs on the highest of thrones
Handsome and glorious
He is the king of this entire world
For without his love
We would be full of sin
We would not be saved or even forgivin
When we die
We will go to be with our king
We will all be angels and we will sing
We should pray right now
Let's ask to be free of doubt and sin
He will come again soon
And he will love us until the end

"Heaven"

Refreshed and relaxed
Fluffy is this cloud
I sit up here happily
Sway and rock
Sing and hum
But not too loud
Wings are near
White pearls shimmer
The voices of angels I hear
Soft and sweet
God is watching us
The feeling is so neat
We just float away
Angelic I feel in my heart
I shall not doubt
I love all day

Precious are our memories
Close our eyes
Think back and see
Fall off the cloud
In time you will
Listen close
You will hear the sound
Beautiful glitter everywhere
Dancing with the angels
Golden sparkles in their hair
We will be protected
From now until we go there
For good we shall stay
No more going back to our old way

"Free Shells"

Warm sand on the bottom of my feet
Salty, Cool water touching the tips of my toes
The wind blows me to the ground
I rest on my knees and think of the past
My life has changed, And keeps on changing
I get up off the warm sand and I take a stroll
I'm on the boardwalk looking at all the sites
I notice sea shells in the windows of the stores
I choose to pick up my own shells off of the ground
Why do people charge for what God gave us for free?
I love the ocean and all of the beauty it gleams
You don't need to pay for the simple things
All of the true glorious things in life are free

"Stranded"

Foggy over marshes below
We drive over the bridge
We don't go very fast
Instead we go really slow
We turned right into the sand
Who now has the upper hand?
I sit and don't make a sound
We are so lost
The fog is hiding us
Will we ever be found?
We need some more light
It soon will be the darkest night
Do you see anything ahead?
I want to go back home
I want to be snug and warm in my bed
Scary is this silent marsh
How did this happen?
I don't like this road at all
Someone is coming this way
He has long brown hair
He says he's been traveling all day

He has a truck that can pull us out
Helping others is what life is all about
He has very bright headlights
We can finally see what has been our unknown sights
We will head back home
To be in the place where we belong
We shouldn't have run away
When we get home
What will we tell them, what will we say
We should have been thankful for what we had
Our lives were not that bad
We just were in a slump and feeling sad
Now we can say thanks to the nice guy
We should really be thankful that he happened to drive by
I hope we can think first next time
God will forgive us for being ungrateful
He has taught us a valuable lesson
We need to do a little less talk and a little more confessing

"Dark to Light"

Misunderstood is my bleeding heart
Understand that I'm not together
I'm rather torn far apart
Asking for what is right
I no longer choose to fight
I'm leaning sideways
Spinning around and around
Hold on real tight
Shaken me up
Turned me upside down
All through the night
I hear the disturbing sound
On my knees I pray
Forgive me again
I will now walk away
Shed the new light
Look upon my tender face
My feelings of hope I will embrace
Shining bright I now see
For the darkness has faded and left me

"Foggy mind"

Dwindling on a downward spiral
Sitting on the edge of desire
Hopping around on thoughts
Standing in the middle of everything
Chasing dreams with one eye open
Staring into the stars ahead
Twinkle goes the one up above
My mind so foggy
Bowing down to the controller
Scared to walk forward
Come to me and see the light
Darkness becomes her reality
Angels are among us all
Waving around us and protecting us
Loving the wrong ones
Doubting the right ones
Praying for peace
Forgive us
A resolution will come

"Window of Heaven"

Staring out of the stained glass window
I see the rain pouring heavily to the ground
The lightening strikes several times
I can hear the banging and rumbling sound
The thunder comes and goes like the rain
I feel somber and content from the sights
My heart still feels that burning pain
I continue to stare out of the window
I try to stay solid as a rock in my mind
I'm not the giving up kind
The sand kicks up and starts to fly to the side
I pray for no twisters to come to take me for a ride
I was put on this earth for a reason I'm sure
I have so much love to give
My love is strong and pure

The rain slows and it becomes a light sprinkle
There are many stars in the sky
Only one of them is mine and it gives me a twinkle
I won't let go of my many dreams
It is time now for me to be redeemed
The rain has stopped altogether
I see my future glimpse in front of me
I'm going to heaven and I will be there forever

"Sail to freedom"

What is wrong with some people today?
They seem to have nothing more nice to say
I can't bare to see homeless people on the street
It bothers me to know that some have no socks or shoes on their feet
When I think, I seem to think deep
My sanity and kindness, I'd like to keep
Why do some people hurt others so bad?
The way the world is now, It all is so very sad
I pray to God every day
Keep this world safe from those who don't obey
I take a deep breath and look in the mirror
I see myself and I have no more fear
I know who I have become
I know I can help this world prevail
I will get on my freedom ship to save others and simply sail
Then I will be able to fully exhale

"1, 2, 3"
"Party for peace"

One, Two, Three, Who do you see?
Four, five, six, Does your Dr. ever fix?
Seven, eight, nine, Does your heart feel divine?
How divine can you really feel?
I love life, Do you love life?
Are you a husband or a devoted wife?
If neither, that's quite ok
We all have our own words that we like to say
Do you treasure anyone who is different?
I do, I love all who are people
They are all very different
My heart can hold more than a ton
I love every person, not just a single one
If we all learn to give and love more
We can open up another door
I don't care if you are stinking rich, or plum poor
Let's all get together and party to the core
Let's party for peace, love, and happiness

"Higher power"

Take that first step
Don't be a snob or prep
Follow your dreams
Don't fall into the fast flowing streams
Chase your devotion
Don't put your life in slow motion
Believe in the higher power
Don't become broken and act sour
Fly to the sunset
Don't turn your back on things you haven't seen yet
Take that small chance
Don't pretend you can't dance
You should be your own best friend
Don't disregard your letters you never wanted to send
Tell people how you really feel
Don't act like you can find a better deal
Try to stay up beat and satisfied
Don't pout and think that everyone has lied
Place your mind in another life
Don't say you will never be a husband or a wife
Talk to God with your heart wide open
Don't be depressed and keep on moping
You are the only one who can change you
Don't ever forget that God makes dreams come true

"Listen"

SSShhh . . . . Quiet
Listen to the wind
Hear the howling
See the moon glow
Feel the invisible compassion
The crickets are playing there trumpets
Beautiful music we can enjoy
The sound spectrum is glorious
Let the spirit surround you
May your sorrow be removed
Watch your sadness disappear
Throw your arms up to the sky
Reach for those glistening stars
Shine, Oh yes they will
The earth is so wonderful and round
Taste the sweetness of the clouds
Pretend you are in them
Close your eyes
Rise above all of your difficult decisions
Talk to your maker
Share your concerns that are nagging you
Take this precious time
Never turn your back on true love
SSShhh . . . . Quiet
Let the love in your heart
And let your mind be free

"Dance and Sing"

My pedals tap on the ground
All I hear is the clip clop sound
Dancing in the rain and thunder
No umbrella for me to stand under
Singing my heart out
I love to feel what life is all about
Raise my hands up to the sky
I see the stars and the moon collide
Taste the drops of rain on my tongue
I will smile and sing those songs that have not yet been sung
Fireflies chase me back in to the house
I will trick them and sneak quietly back out
You can't keep me from mother nature
I love every animal, bug or creature
My life consists of exploring new beings
Take chances and you can accomplish many things
Keep heading for that shiny star
Don't fall down
Hold on tight to your dream bar

"To be my friend"

Don't pick your nose in public, It is so rude
I don't like your language either, It's quite crude
Your smells are, cigarettes and tar
You smell like you just walked out of a nasty bar
My faith keeps me loving everyone though
I love people who I don't even know
I wish you would refrain from saying awful things
To be my friend, You don't need to wear diamond rings
Take a step in my direction
I can assure you, You'll get hugs and affection
You seem to be seeking a hand to hold
You don't need to be so loud or bold
Change your attitude just a little bit
You can have all kinds of nice friends
That is all you need to do, That is it
Just be more friendly to your neighbor
I think you need some faith in your life
Talk to your maker and don't even think twice
You need to be saved and put in your right place
It would be nice to see a big smile on your face
So, don't look down
Look up to the sky
Don't frown or even make a sigh
You can make it to where you want to be
Close your eyes and dream
When you open your eyes, make your dream real
Let out those harsh feelings that you feel
As a friend, I shall protect you always
Stand tall and believe in yourself
I won't let you fail, drown or fall
Trust in your heart and in your mind
Leave your old worries and past behind

"Be A Leader"

Life is funny, I think to myself
The way some things happen
I wonder still, Why certain things do happen
I do, however believe in God
I know he has a plan for the way things turn out
I should not ask God why he does things
He must have his reasoning
I will keep my faith steady and firm
My heart open to miracles
I will trust in his word and works
I will always be a believer and a follower
In life, I'm a leader as well as a follower
I do what I believe and love what I know
I only follow my heart, Not other people
The rainbows we see after rain, They are miracles
A new born baby is a miracle
I wish everyone would follow there hearts
This world would be much more joyful
I look up to see a falling star
To me, That even is a miracle
Whatever you believe, It must be what you want to believe
Don't let others change how you really feel
Follow your true heart and true feelings
Don't be a follower to other people
Be brave and strong, Stick up for what you believe
Be a leader in your own life

"My faith is forever"

Forever faithful I will walk this path
Bouncing and jiggling off of the high grass
There is no rain in heavens sight
Beautiful it shall be on this very night
The moon glows like a big round night light
I skip in circles to envision Gods light
I will always do holy things to thrive in my life
Singing lullabies straight to the sky
I will do everything in my power to succeed and fly
I love this path that I walk everyday
It gives me more pleasure than I can say
My heart beats so fast out of my chest
I love this life that I was given
So, I will give back to life and do my very best